BOAS

Sierra Wilson

The World of Snakes

www.av2books.com

Step 1
Go to **www.av2books.com**

Step 2
Enter this unique code

JRBKQQ7YM

Step 3
Explore your interactive eBook!

AV2 is optimized for use on any device

Your interactive eBook comes with...

Contents
Browse a live contents page to easily navigate through resources

Audio
Listen to sections of the book read aloud

Videos
Watch informative video clips

Weblinks
Gain additional information for research

Slideshows
View images and captions

Try This!
Complete activities and hands-on experiments

Key Words
Study vocabulary, and complete a matching word activity

Quizzes
Test your knowledge

Share
Share titles within your Learning Management System (LMS) or Library Circulation System

Citation
Create bibliographical references following the Chicago Manual of Style

This title is part of our AV2 digital subscription

1-Year 3–8 Subscription
ISBN 978-1-7911-3306-1

Access hundreds of AV2 titles with our digital subscription.
Sign up for a FREE trial at **www.av2books.com/trial**

BOAS

CONTENTS

Large Constrictors

The name *boa* means "large snake" in Latin. Boas are big, powerful snakes from the boid **family**. They include the heaviest snakes on Earth. There are more than 40 **species** of boas.

Like all snakes, boas are reptiles. This means they breathe air and have bony plates called scales on their bodies. They also use their surroundings to warm up.

WARNING

A large boa can be dangerous. Using its body, it can squeeze a person hard enough to **stop his or her blood from flowing**.

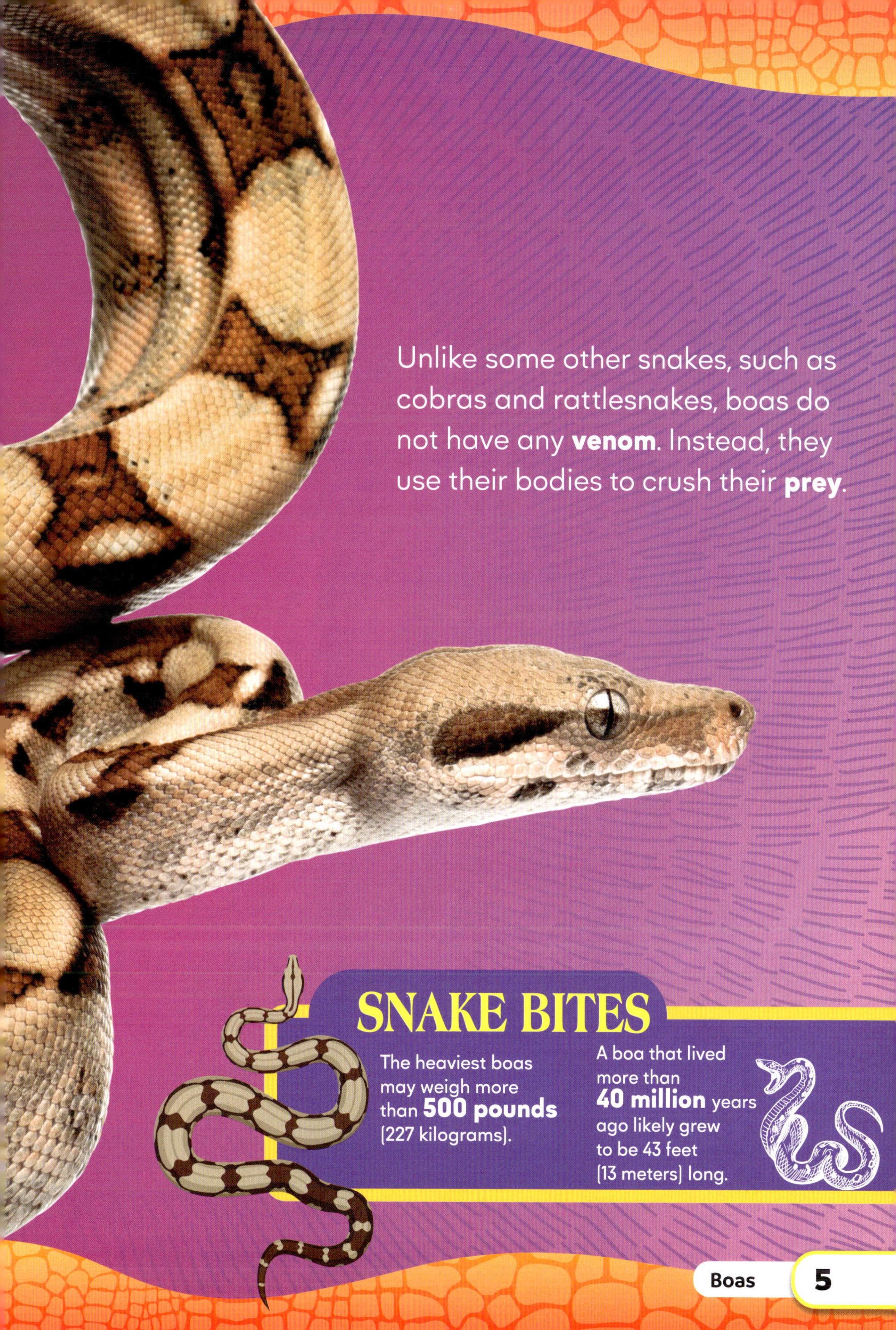

Unlike some other snakes, such as cobras and rattlesnakes, boas do not have any **venom**. Instead, they use their bodies to crush their **prey**.

SNAKE BITES

The heaviest boas may weigh more than **500 pounds** (227 kilograms).

A boa that lived more than **40 million** years ago likely grew to be 43 feet (13 meters) long.

What Do Boas Look Like?

Boas are known for their long, thick, powerful bodies. These snakes are usually 3 to 15 feet (1 to 4.5 m) long. However, the largest boas, such as green anacondas, may grow longer than 20 feet (6 m).

Measuring Up

Average snake lengths

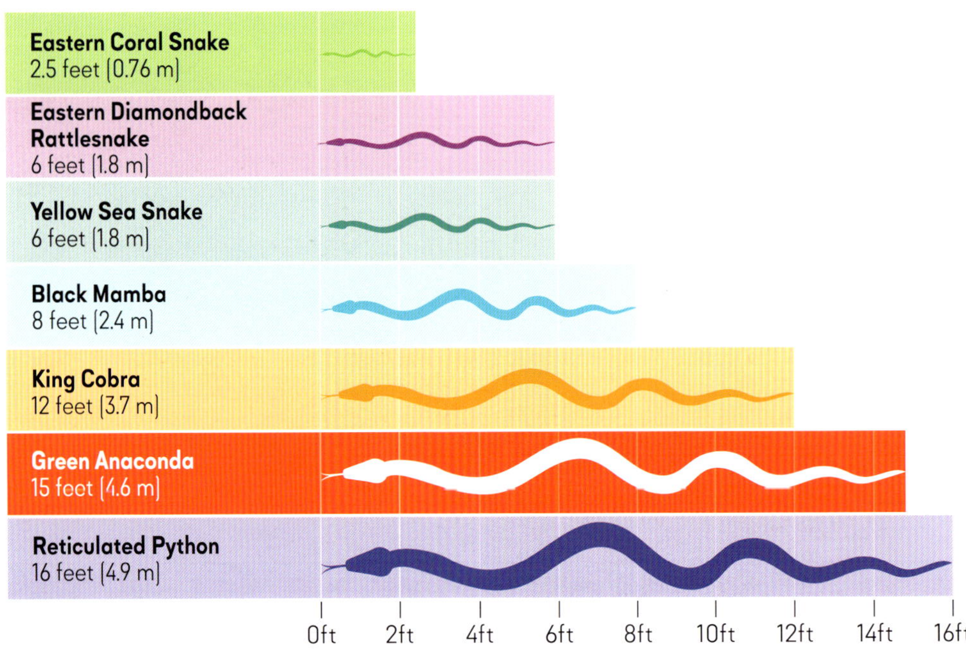

Boas come in many colors and patterns. They may have orange, brown, green, or yellow scales. Several have black and brown markings, such as spots and bands. Often, boas have coloring that matches their environment. This **camouflage** allows them to hide while waiting for prey. Certain species of boa change color due to the time of day or the season.

Other boas have scales with unusual textures. The rubber boa, found in the United States and Canada, has smooth, shiny scales, making it feel rubbery. Ridges on a rainbow boa's scales make them shimmer.

The Life Cycle

Like all living things, boas have a life cycle. A boa will be born, grow, and **reproduce**. Boas may live more than 30 years.

1

Unlike most other snakes, boas do not lay eggs. Instead, a boa mother gives birth to 8 to 50 live young.

2

Baby boas can care for themselves from the moment they are born. They are born knowing how to hunt and stay safe.

3

Young boas spend much of their time in trees. As they grow, they shed their skin.

4

At around 3 years of age, boas are ready to find a **mate**. Adult male boas flick their tongues to follow the scent of a female. Several males may wrestle to compete for a mate.

A Boa's Body

Like all living things, a boa has many different **adaptations**. Some keep the snake safe. Others help it to survive in its **habitat**.

Teeth
Boas have curved teeth, like hooks, that help them hold onto their prey.

Heat Pits
Many boas have small holes near their mouth that help them sense body heat from their prey.

Belly Scales
Boas do not slither. Scales on their bellies help them grip the ground and move in a straight line.

Jaw
A boa's jaw has stretchy **ligaments** that allow it to open very wide to swallow animals whole.

Where Boas Live

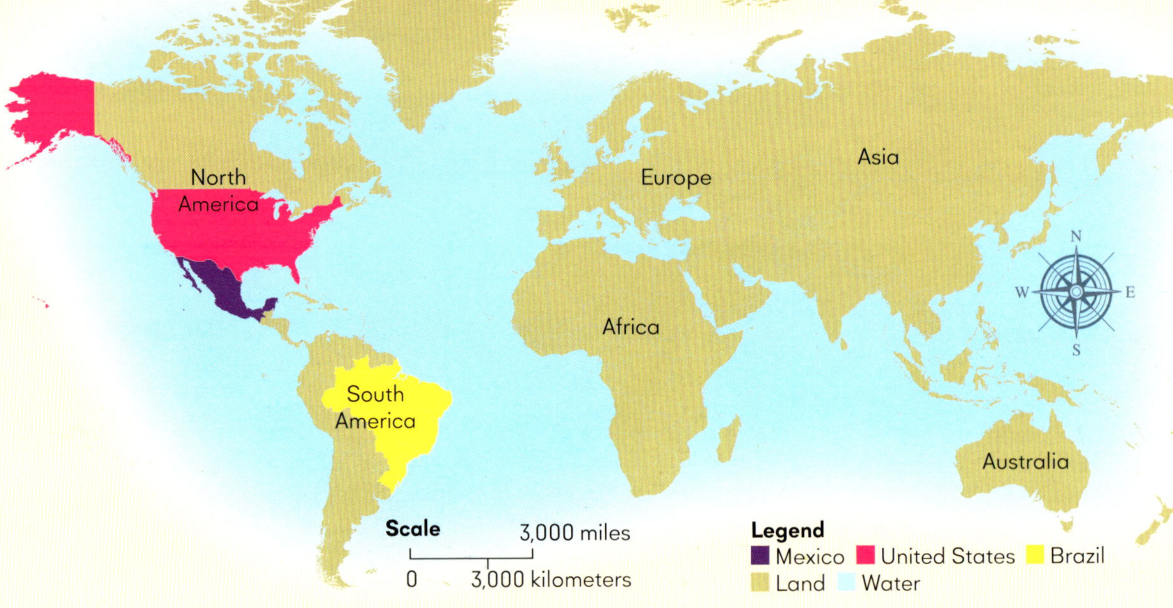

Most boas live in North and South America. However, they can be found on every continent except for Antarctica. Boas live in many habitats. Boas live in rainforests, grasslands, wetlands, deserts, and forests.

Boa Range

Africa, Asia, North America, South America, Australia, Europe

Boa Habitats

Desert, Forest, Grassland, Rainforest, Wetland

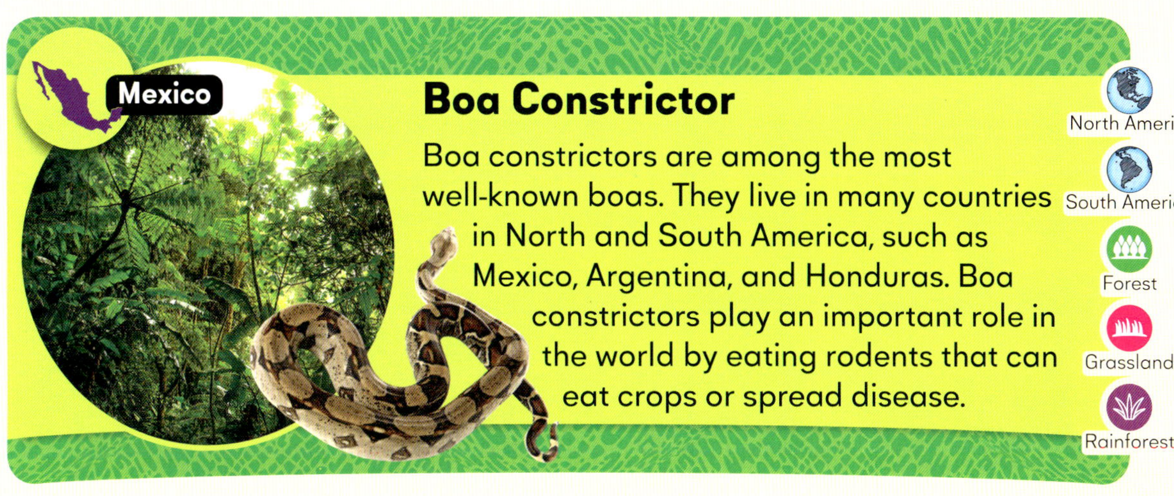

Boa Constrictor

Boa constrictors are among the most well-known boas. They live in many countries in North and South America, such as Mexico, Argentina, and Honduras. Boa constrictors play an important role in the world by eating rodents that can eat crops or spread disease.

Rosy Boa

The rosy boa is one of the smaller boas. These snakes come in many patterns. Some have pink scales, giving the species its name. Rosy boas live in the southwestern United States and Mexico. They spend most of their lives hiding under rocks. Rosy boas rarely bite, which has helped make them popular pets.

Green Anaconda

Green anacondas are the heaviest snakes on Earth. They live in swamps, wetlands, rivers, and streams in tropical areas of South America such as Brazil, Venezuela, and Colombia. Their eyes and nostrils are on top of their heads, so they can hide in water and wait for prey. They wrap their prey in their **coils** and drown it.

On the Hunt

Boas hide to wait for food. Sometimes, they lurk in trees, near caves, or in water. When prey passes by, they **ambush** it. Boas bite the animal and quickly wrap it in their coils. Then, they squeeze the animal tightly. This is called constricting. Finally, boas swallow their prey whole.

After eating, boas can go for weeks or even months without needing food.

Boas eat anything they can catch and swallow, including bats, birds, rodents, monkeys, deer, and even jaguars. It takes several days for boas to **digest** a meal. Strong stomach acid helps boas digest any animals they eat.

Kenyan sand boas hunt by hiding their bodies under the sand in deserts.

Keeping Safe

Even though boas are often large and strong, they still face **predators**. Younger and smaller boas are especially at risk. Predators of boas include birds, foxes, and crocodiles.

When faced with a predator, boas try to hide. They stay very still to blend in with their surroundings. If that does not work, they may hiss as a warning, let out a stinky odor, or bite.

Some boas have tails that look very similar to their heads. These snakes may use their tails to confuse predators.

Depending on the size of the animals, jaguars and anacondas may prey on each other.

Threats to Boas

Like all living things, boas face many challenges such as habitat loss, climate change, and human behavior. Cutting down forests destroys many boas' homes. As forests are cut down for lumber or to make room for farms, there are fewer places for boas to live.

Boas are also threatened by hunting. They are hunted for meat and to use their skin as leather. Other boas are captured to be sold as pets.

In 2020, about 5 million acres (2 million hectares) of the Amazon Rainforest was lost. This area is home to many boas, including green anacondas.

Several boa species are **endangered**, **vulnerable**, or decreasing. One species of boa, the Conception Bank silver boa, is critically endangered. Several countries and groups are working together to protect this snake from **extinction**.

Mona boas are only found on Mona Island, west of Puerto Rico.

The Mona boa is another endangered species. People are working to rebuild the Mona boa **population** by breeding new snakes in places such as zoos, then placing them back in their natural habitats.

SNAKE BITES

There are **fewer than 1,000** adult Conception Bank silver boas alive today.

The Mona boa was declared to be endangered **in 1996**.

ACTIVITY
Create a Snake

There are many different kinds of snakes in the world. They all have certain features in common. However, each snake also has its own unique features. They help the snake live in its home.

Make your own snake by answering the following questions:

1. What is your snake called?
2. Where does it live?
3. What features does it share with other snakes?
4. What features help it live in its home? How do these features do this?
5. What does your snake look like?
6. Use a pencil or pen to draw your snake living in its home. Make sure to include all of its features.

Supplies needed
for this activity
Pencil
or pen
Paper
Eraser

BOA QUIZ

How well do you know your boas? Take this short quiz to find out.

1. How many species of boa are there?
2. How long can a boa live?
3. Which boa is known for its rubbery-feeling body?
4. Why are boa teeth curved like hooks?
5. Where do green anacondas often hide?
6. How long can boas go without food?
7. What are some ways in which boas defend themselves?
8. Which species of boa is critically endangered?

ANSWERS

1. More than 40 **2.** More than 30 years **3.** The rubber boa **4.** To help boas hold onto prey **5.** In the water **6.** Weeks or months **7.** Hide, hiss, make an odor, or bite **8.** The Conception Bank silver boa

Key Words

adaptations: changes in animals or plants that make them better able to survive in their homes

ambush: to attack by surprise

camouflage: a natural disguise

coils: a loop of something that wraps around

digest: to break down food inside the body

endangered: close to becoming extinct

extinction: when a group of animals or plants no longer exists

family: a group of living things that share certain characteristics

habitat: the place where a plant or animal lives

ligaments: flexible tissue in the body that connects things

mate: a member of a pair of animals that can reproduce or have babies

population: the number of animals in a certain group or area

predators: animals that hunt other animals

prey: animals that are hunted by other animals

reproduce: to have babies

species: a group of closely related animals or plants

venom: a toxic chemical produced by some animals

vulnerable: likely to become endangered soon

Index

Get the best of both worlds.

AV2 bridges the gap between print and digital.

The expandable resources toolbar enables quick access to content including **videos**, **audio**, **activities**, **weblinks**, **slideshows**, **quizzes**, and **key words**.

Animated videos make static images come alive.

Resource icons on each page help readers to further **explore key concepts**.

Published by AV2
276 5th Avenue
Suite 704 #917
New York, NY 10001
Website: www.av2books.com

Library of Congress Control Number: 2021940096

ISBN 978-1-7911-4154-7 (hardcover)
ISBN 978-1-7911-4155-4 (softcover)
ISBN 978-1-7911-4156-1 (multi-user eBook)

Printed in Guangzhou, China
1 2 3 4 5 6 7 8 9 0 25 24 23 22 21

062021
101120

Art Director: Terry Paulhus Project Coordinator: John Willis

Every reasonable effort has been made to trace ownership and to obtain permission to reprint copyright material. The publisher would be pleased to have any errors or omissions brought to its attention so that they may be corrected in subsequent printings.

The publisher acknowledges Alamy, Getty Images, Minden Pictures, and Shutterstock as the primary image suppliers for this title.